Hea_____th

Grains

Nancy Dickmann

D0005587

Heinemann
LIBRARY

Chicago, Illinois

www.capstonepub.com
Visit our website to find out more information about Heinemann-Raintree books.

To order:

☎ Phone 888-454-2279

⌨ Visit www.capstonepub.com to browse our catalog and order online.

©2012 Heinemann Library
an imprint of Capstone Global Library, LLC
Chicago, Illinois

Edited by Rebecca Rissman and Adrian Vigliano
Designed by Joanna Hinton-Malivoire
Original Illustrations © Capstone Global Library Ltd 2010
Illustrated by Tony Wilson
Picture research by Elizabeth Alexander
Production by Victoria Fitzgerald
Originated by Capstone Global Library Ltd
Printed in the United States of America by Worzalla Publishing.

15 14 13 12 11
10 9 8 7 6 5 4 3 2 1

Library of Congress Cataloging-in-Publication Data
Cataloging-in-Publication data is on file at the Library of Congress.

ISBN 978-1-4329-6975-2 (hc) -- ISBN 978-1-4329-6982-0 (pb)

Acknowledgments
We would like to thank the following for permission to reproduce photographs: Capstone Publishers p.22 (© Karon Dubke); Corbis p.21 (© Roy McMahon); Getty Images pp.8 (White Rock/DAJ), 12 (Tanya Constantine/Photographer's Choice), 17 (Tara Moore/Taxi); Photolibrary pp.5 (Emely/Cultura), 6 (Gilles Rouget/Photononstop); Shutterstock pp.4, 23 bottom (© Elena Elisseeva), 7 main (© MarFot), 7 inset (© Petrenko Andriy), 9 (© iwka), 10 (© Morgan Lane Photography), 11 (© Victoria Visuals), 13, 23 top (© Monkey Business Images), 14 (© 6493866629), 15 (© Mikus, Jo.), 16 (© Nic Neish) 18 (© Flashon Studio), 20 (© paulaphoto); U.S. Department of Agriculture, Center for Nutrition Policy and Promotion p.19.

Front cover photograph of grains group reproduced with permission of Shutterstock (© Morgan Lane Photography). Back cover photograph of a girl eating cereal reproduced with permission of Corbis (© Roy McMahon).

Every effort has been made to contact copyright holders of material reproduced in this book. Any omissions will be rectified in subsequent printings if notice is given to the publishers.

Contents

What Are Grains?. 4

Food from Grains. 8

How Grains Help Us 12

Healthy Eating 18

Find the Grains 22

Picture Glossary. 23

Index 24

What Are Grains?

seeds

Grains are the seeds from some plants.

Eating grains can keep us healthy.

wheat

rice

Wheat and rice are grains.

oats

Oats are grains.

Food from Grains

rice

We cook some grains before eating.

flour

We make some grains into flour.

pasta

bread

Bread and pasta are made
from flour.

tortilla

Some tortillas are made from flour.

How Grains Help Us

Eating grains gives you energy.

You need energy to work and play.

part of the grain

Some foods are made with part of the grain.

whole grain

Some foods are made with the whole grain.

Eating whole grains helps your body fight illness.

Eating whole grains helps keep your heart healthy.

Healthy Eating

We need to eat different kinds of food each day.

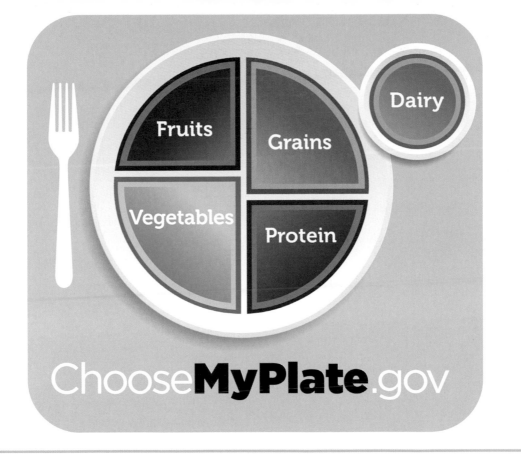

MyPlate reminds us to eat some foods from each food group every day.

We eat grains to stay healthy.

We eat grains because they taste good!

Find the Grains

Here is a healthy dinner. Can you find a food made from grains?

Answer on page 24

Picture Glossary

energy the power to do something. We need energy when we work or play.

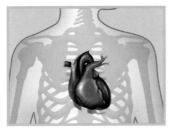

heart part of your body inside your chest. Your heart pushes blood around your body.

seed plants make seeds. Seeds grow into new plants. We can eat some seeds.

Index

energy 12, 13

flour 9, 10, 11

MyPlate 19

oats 7

rice 6, 8

seeds 4

wheat 6

whole grain 15–17

Answer to quiz on page 22: The bread is made from grains.

Notes for parents and teachers

Before reading

Explain that we need to eat a range of different foods to stay healthy. Splitting foods into different groups can help us understand how much food we should eat from each group. Introduce the grains element in the MyPlate graphic on page 19. Grains are seeds from plants. Eating grains gives us energy.

After reading

• Play "Spot the grains." Take children around a supermarket in small groups and ask them to draw or record all the grains they see. Alternatively, hold up pictures of different types of food and ask the children whether they think grains are being shown in each picture.

• Discuss the difference between foods made with whole grain (literally the entire grain kernel) such as whole wheat bread, and foods where part of the grain has been removed, such as white flour, white bread, and white rice. Explain that whole grain foods are much better for us. Bring in three different types of whole wheat bread (checking that no children have gluten or nut allergies). Conduct a taste test to see which kind of bread is the favorite.

• Help the children to each design a healthy lunch (or lunch box). Discuss the sorts of things that might go into a healthy lunch and the importance of including a range of different types of food. What grains are they going to include? The lunches could be drawn on paper plates and displayed along with an illustrated drink for each meal.